THESE RECIPES BELONG TO :

_____

_____

My Recipes Table of Contents

01	
02	
03	
04	
05	
06	
07	
08	
09	
10	
11	
12	
13	
14	
15	
16	
17	
18	
19	
20	

My Recipes Table of Contents

21	
22	
23	
24	
25	
26	
27	
28	
29	
30	
31	
32	
33	
34	
35	
36	
37	
38	
39	
40	

My Recipes Table of Contents

41	
42	
43	
44	
45	
46	
47	
48	
49	
50	
51	
52	
53	
54	
55	
56	
57	
58	
59	
60	

My Recipes Table of Contents

61	
62	
63	
64	
65	
66	
67	
68	
69	
70	
71	
72	
73	
74	
75	
76	
77	
78	
79	
80	

My Recipes Table of Contents

81	
82	
83	
84	
85	
86	
87	
88	
89	
90	
91	
92	
93	
94	
95	
96	
97	
98	
99	
100	

RECIPE: .... FROM: ....

SERVINGS: ...... PREP TIME: .... COOK TIME:.......... OVEN TEMP: ....

INGREDIENTS: _____

_____

_____

_____

_____

_____

_____

_____

_____

_____

_____

_____

_____

INSTRUCTIONS: _____

_____

_____

_____

_____

_____

_____

_____

_____

_____

_____

_____

RECIPE: .... FROM: ....

SERVINGS: ...... PREP TIME: .... COOK TIME:.......... OVEN TEMP: ....

INGREDIENTS: _____

_____

_____

_____

_____

_____

_____

_____

_____

_____

_____

_____

_____

_____

INSTRUCTIONS: _____

_____

_____

_____

_____

_____

_____

_____

_____

_____

_____

_____

_____

RECIPE: .... FROM: ....

SERVINGS: ...... PREP TIME: .... COOK TIME:.......... OVEN TEMP: ....

INGREDIENTS: _____

_____

_____

_____

_____

_____

_____

_____

_____

_____

_____

_____

_____

_____

_____

_____

INSTRUCTIONS: _____

_____

_____

_____

_____

_____

_____

_____

_____

_____

_____

_____

_____

_____

RECIPE: .... FROM: ....

SERVINGS: ...... PREP TIME: .... COOK TIME:.......... OVEN TEMP: ....

INGREDIENTS: _____

_____
_____
_____
_____
_____
_____
_____
_____
_____
_____
_____
_____
_____
_____
_____

INSTRUCTIONS: _____

_____
_____
_____
_____
_____
_____
_____
_____
_____
_____
_____
_____
_____
_____
_____

RECIPE: .... FROM: ....

SERVINGS: ...... PREP TIME: .... COOK TIME:.......... OVEN TEMP: ....

INGREDIENTS: _____

_____

_____

_____

_____

_____

_____

_____

_____

_____

_____

_____

_____

_____

_____

_____

INSTRUCTIONS: _____

_____

_____

_____

_____

_____

_____

_____

_____

_____

_____

_____

_____

_____

_____

RECIPE: .... FROM: ....

SERVINGS: ...... PREP TIME: .... COOK TIME:.......... OVEN TEMP: ....

INGREDIENTS: _____

_____
_____
_____
_____
_____
_____
_____
_____
_____
_____
_____
_____
_____

INSTRUCTIONS: _____

_____
_____
_____
_____
_____
_____
_____
_____
_____
_____
_____
_____
_____

RECIPE: .... FROM: ....

SERVINGS: ...... PREP TIME: .... COOK TIME:.......... OVEN TEMP: ....

INGREDIENTS: _____

_____

_____

_____

_____

_____

_____

_____

_____

_____

_____

_____

_____

_____

_____

INSTRUCTIONS: _____

_____

_____

_____

_____

_____

_____

_____

_____

_____

_____

_____

_____

_____

RECIPE: .... FROM: ....

SERVINGS: ...... PREP TIME: .... COOK TIME:.......... OVEN TEMP: ....

INGREDIENTS: _____

_____
_____
_____
_____
_____
_____
_____
_____
_____
_____
_____
_____
_____
_____

INSTRUCTIONS: _____

_____
_____
_____
_____
_____
_____
_____
_____
_____
_____
_____
_____
_____

RECIPE: .... FROM: ....

SERVINGS: ...... PREP TIME: .... COOK TIME:.......... OVEN TEMP: ....

INGREDIENTS: _____

_____

_____

_____

_____

_____

_____

_____

_____

_____

_____

_____

_____

INSTRUCTIONS: _____

_____

_____

_____

_____

_____

_____

_____

_____

_____

_____

_____

_____

RECIPE: .... FROM: ....

SERVINGS: ...... PREP TIME: .... COOK TIME:.......... OVEN TEMP: ....

INGREDIENTS: _____

_____

_____

_____

_____

_____

_____

_____

_____

_____

_____

_____

_____

INSTRUCTIONS: _____

_____

_____

_____

_____

_____

_____

_____

_____

_____

_____

_____

RECIPE: .... FROM: ....

SERVINGS: ...... PREP TIME: .... COOK TIME:.......... OVEN TEMP: ....

INGREDIENTS: _____

_____

_____

_____

_____

_____

_____

_____

_____

_____

_____

_____

_____

INSTRUCTIONS: _____

_____

_____

_____

_____

_____

_____

_____

_____

_____

_____

_____

_____

RECIPE: .... FROM: ....

SERVINGS: ...... PREP TIME: .... COOK TIME:......... OVEN TEMP: ....

INGREDIENTS: _____

_____
_____
_____
_____
_____
_____
_____
_____
_____
_____
_____
_____
_____

INSTRUCTIONS: _____

_____
_____
_____
_____
_____
_____
_____
_____
_____
_____
_____
_____
_____
_____

RECIPE: .... FROM: ....

SERVINGS: ...... PREP TIME: .... COOK TIME:.......... OVEN TEMP: ....

INGREDIENTS: _____

_____

_____

_____

_____

_____

_____

_____

_____

_____

_____

_____

_____

INSTRUCTIONS: _____

_____

_____

_____

_____

_____

_____

_____

_____

_____

_____

_____

RECIPE: .... FROM: ....

SERVINGS: ...... PREP TIME: .... COOK TIME:......... OVEN TEMP: ....

INGREDIENTS: _____

_____
_____
_____
_____
_____
_____
_____
_____
_____
_____
_____
_____

INSTRUCTIONS: _____

_____
_____
_____
_____
_____
_____
_____
_____
_____
_____
_____
_____

RECIPE: .... FROM: ....

SERVINGS: ...... PREP TIME: .... COOK TIME:.......... OVEN TEMP: ....

INGREDIENTS: _____

_____

_____

_____

_____

_____

_____

_____

_____

_____

_____

_____

_____

_____

INSTRUCTIONS: _____

_____

_____

_____

_____

_____

_____

_____

_____

_____

_____

_____

RECIPE: .... FROM: ....

SERVINGS: ...... PREP TIME: .... COOK TIME:.......... OVEN TEMP: ....

INGREDIENTS: _____

_____
_____
_____
_____
_____
_____
_____
_____
_____
_____
_____
_____
_____
_____

INSTRUCTIONS: _____

_____
_____
_____
_____
_____
_____
_____
_____
_____
_____
_____
_____
_____

RECIPE: .... FROM: ....

SERVINGS: ...... PREP TIME: .... COOK TIME:.......... OVEN TEMP: ....

INGREDIENTS: _____

_____

_____

_____

_____

_____

_____

_____

_____

_____

_____

_____

_____

_____

INSTRUCTIONS: _____

_____

_____

_____

_____

_____

_____

_____

_____

_____

_____

_____

_____

_____

_____

RECIPE: .... FROM: ....

SERVINGS: ...... PREP TIME: .... COOK TIME:.......... OVEN TEMP: ....

INGREDIENTS: _____

_____

_____

_____

_____

_____

_____

_____

_____

_____

_____

_____

_____

_____

_____

INSTRUCTIONS: _____

_____

_____

_____

_____

_____

_____

_____

_____

_____

_____

_____

_____

_____

RECIPE: .... FROM: ....

SERVINGS: ...... PREP TIME: .... COOK TIME:.......... OVEN TEMP: ....

INGREDIENTS: _____

_____

_____

_____

_____

_____

_____

_____

_____

_____

_____

_____

_____

_____

INSTRUCTIONS: _____

_____

_____

_____

_____

_____

_____

_____

_____

_____

_____

_____

_____

RECIPE: .... FROM: ....

SERVINGS: ...... PREP TIME: .... COOK TIME:.......... OVEN TEMP: ....

INGREDIENTS: _____

_____

_____

_____

_____

_____

_____

_____

_____

_____

_____

_____

_____

_____

_____

INSTRUCTIONS: _____

_____

_____

_____

_____

_____

_____

_____

_____

_____

_____

_____

_____

_____

RECIPE: .... FROM: ....

SERVINGS: ...... PREP TIME: .... COOK TIME:.......... OVEN TEMP: ....

INGREDIENTS: _____

_____

_____

_____

_____

_____

_____

_____

_____

_____

_____

_____

_____

_____

INSTRUCTIONS: _____

_____

_____

_____

_____

_____

_____

_____

_____

_____

_____

_____

_____

RECIPE: .... FROM: ....

SERVINGS: ...... PREP TIME: .... COOK TIME:.......... OVEN TEMP: ....

INGREDIENTS: _____

_____
_____
_____
_____
_____
_____
_____
_____
_____
_____
_____
_____
_____
_____

INSTRUCTIONS: _____

_____
_____
_____
_____
_____
_____
_____
_____
_____
_____
_____
_____

RECIPE: .... FROM: ....

SERVINGS: ...... PREP TIME: .... COOK TIME:.......... OVEN TEMP: ....

INGREDIENTS: _____

_____

_____

_____

_____

_____

_____

_____

_____

_____

_____

_____

_____

_____

INSTRUCTIONS: _____

_____

_____

_____

_____

_____

_____

_____

_____

_____

_____

_____

_____

RECIPE: .... FROM: ....

SERVINGS: ...... PREP TIME: .... COOK TIME:.......... OVEN TEMP: ....

INGREDIENTS: _____

_____
_____
_____
_____
_____
_____
_____
_____
_____
_____
_____
_____
_____

INSTRUCTIONS: _____

_____
_____
_____
_____
_____
_____
_____
_____
_____
_____
_____
_____
_____

RECIPE: .... FROM: ....

SERVINGS: ...... PREP TIME: .... COOK TIME:.......... OVEN TEMP: ....

INGREDIENTS: _____

_____
_____
_____
_____
_____
_____
_____
_____
_____
_____
_____
_____
_____
_____

INSTRUCTIONS: _____

_____
_____
_____
_____
_____
_____
_____
_____
_____
_____
_____
_____
_____
_____

RECIPE: .... FROM: ....

SERVINGS: ...... PREP TIME: .... COOK TIME:.......... OVEN TEMP: ....

INGREDIENTS: _____

_____
_____
_____
_____
_____
_____
_____
_____
_____
_____
_____
_____
_____

INSTRUCTIONS: _____

_____
_____
_____
_____
_____
_____
_____
_____
_____
_____
_____
_____
_____

RECIPE: .... FROM: ....

SERVINGS: ...... PREP TIME: .... COOK TIME:.......... OVEN TEMP: ....

INGREDIENTS: _____

_____

_____

_____

_____

_____

_____

_____

_____

_____

_____

_____

_____

_____

INSTRUCTIONS: _____

_____

_____

_____

_____

_____

_____

_____

_____

_____

_____

_____

RECIPE: .... FROM: ....

SERVINGS: ...... PREP TIME: .... COOK TIME:.......... OVEN TEMP: ....

INGREDIENTS: _____

_____

_____

_____

_____

_____

_____

_____

_____

_____

_____

_____

_____

_____

INSTRUCTIONS: _____

_____

_____

_____

_____

_____

_____

_____

_____

_____

_____

_____

_____

RECIPE: .... FROM: ....

SERVINGS: ...... PREP TIME: .... COOK TIME:.......... OVEN TEMP: ....

INGREDIENTS: _____

_____

_____

_____

_____

_____

_____

_____

_____

_____

_____

_____

_____

_____

_____

INSTRUCTIONS: _____

_____

_____

_____

_____

_____

_____

_____

_____

_____

_____

_____

_____

_____

RECIPE: .... FROM: ....

SERVINGS: ...... PREP TIME: .... COOK TIME:.......... OVEN TEMP: ....

INGREDIENTS: _____

_____

_____

_____

_____

_____

_____

_____

_____

_____

_____

_____

_____

_____

_____

INSTRUCTIONS: _____

_____

_____

_____

_____

_____

_____

_____

_____

_____

_____

_____

_____

_____

RECIPE: .... FROM: ....

SERVINGS: ...... PREP TIME: .... COOK TIME:.......... OVEN TEMP: ....

INGREDIENTS: _____

_____

_____

_____

_____

_____

_____

_____

_____

_____

_____

_____

_____

_____

_____

INSTRUCTIONS: _____

_____

_____

_____

_____

_____

_____

_____

_____

_____

_____

_____

_____

_____

RECIPE: .... FROM: ....

SERVINGS: ...... PREP TIME: .... COOK TIME:.......... OVEN TEMP: ....

INGREDIENTS: _____

_____

_____

_____

_____

_____

_____

_____

_____

_____

_____

_____

_____

INSTRUCTIONS: _____

_____

_____

_____

_____

_____

_____

_____

_____

_____

_____

_____

_____

RECIPE: .... FROM: ....

SERVINGS: ...... PREP TIME: .... COOK TIME:.......... OVEN TEMP: ....

INGREDIENTS: _____

_____
_____
_____
_____
_____
_____
_____
_____
_____
_____
_____
_____

INSTRUCTIONS: _____

_____
_____
_____
_____
_____
_____
_____
_____
_____
_____
_____
_____
_____

RECIPE: .... FROM: ....

SERVINGS: ...... PREP TIME: .... COOK TIME:.......... OVEN TEMP: ....

INGREDIENTS: _____

_____
_____
_____
_____
_____
_____
_____
_____
_____
_____
_____
_____
_____
_____
_____

INSTRUCTIONS: _____

_____
_____
_____
_____
_____
_____
_____
_____
_____
_____
_____
_____
_____
_____

RECIPE: .... FROM: ....

SERVINGS: ...... PREP TIME: .... COOK TIME:.......... OVEN TEMP: ....

INGREDIENTS: _____

_____

_____

_____

_____

_____

_____

_____

_____

_____

_____

_____

_____

_____

_____

_____

INSTRUCTIONS: _____

_____

_____

_____

_____

_____

_____

_____

_____

_____

_____

_____

_____

_____

RECIPE: .... FROM: ....

SERVINGS: ...... PREP TIME: .... COOK TIME:.......... OVEN TEMP: ....

INGREDIENTS: _____

_____
_____
_____
_____
_____
_____
_____
_____
_____
_____
_____
_____
_____

INSTRUCTIONS: _____

_____
_____
_____
_____
_____
_____
_____
_____
_____
_____
_____
_____
_____

RECIPE: .... FROM: ....

SERVINGS: ...... PREP TIME: .... COOK TIME:.......... OVEN TEMP: ....

INGREDIENTS: _____

_____

_____

_____

_____

_____

_____

_____

_____

_____

_____

_____

_____

INSTRUCTIONS: _____

_____

_____

_____

_____

_____

_____

_____

_____

_____

_____

_____

RECIPE: .... FROM: ....

SERVINGS: ...... PREP TIME: .... COOK TIME:.......... OVEN TEMP: ....

INGREDIENTS: _____

_____

_____

_____

_____

_____

_____

_____

_____

_____

_____

_____

_____

_____

INSTRUCTIONS: _____

_____

_____

_____

_____

_____

_____

_____

_____

_____

_____

_____

_____

_____

RECIPE: .... FROM: ....

SERVINGS: ...... PREP TIME: .... COOK TIME:.......... OVEN TEMP: ....

INGREDIENTS: _____

_____

_____

_____

_____

_____

_____

_____

_____

_____

_____

_____

_____

INSTRUCTIONS: _____

_____

_____

_____

_____

_____

_____

_____

_____

_____

_____

_____

_____

_____

RECIPE: .... FROM: ....

SERVINGS: ...... PREP TIME: .... COOK TIME:.......... OVEN TEMP: ....

INGREDIENTS: _____

_____

_____

_____

_____

_____

_____

_____

_____

_____

_____

_____

_____

_____

_____

_____

_____

INSTRUCTIONS: _____

_____

_____

_____

_____

_____

_____

_____

_____

_____

_____

_____

_____

_____

_____

RECIPE: .... FROM: ....

SERVINGS: ...... PREP TIME: .... COOK TIME:.......... OVEN TEMP: ....

INGREDIENTS: _____

_____
_____
_____
_____
_____
_____
_____
_____
_____
_____
_____
_____
_____
_____

INSTRUCTIONS: _____

_____
_____
_____
_____
_____
_____
_____
_____
_____
_____
_____
_____
_____

RECIPE: .... FROM: ....

SERVINGS: ...... PREP TIME: .... COOK TIME:.......... OVEN TEMP: ....

INGREDIENTS: _____

_____
_____
_____
_____
_____
_____
_____
_____
_____
_____
_____
_____
_____
_____

INSTRUCTIONS: _____

_____
_____
_____
_____
_____
_____
_____
_____
_____
_____
_____
_____
_____

RECIPE: .... FROM: ....

SERVINGS: ...... PREP TIME: .... COOK TIME:.......... OVEN TEMP: ....

INGREDIENTS: _____

_____

_____

_____

_____

_____

_____

_____

_____

_____

_____

_____

_____

INSTRUCTIONS: _____

_____

_____

_____

_____

_____

_____

_____

_____

_____

_____

_____

RECIPE: .... FROM: ....

SERVINGS: ...... PREP TIME: .... COOK TIME:.......... OVEN TEMP: ....

INGREDIENTS: _____

_____
_____
_____
_____
_____
_____
_____
_____
_____
_____
_____
_____
_____
_____

INSTRUCTIONS: _____

_____
_____
_____
_____
_____
_____
_____
_____
_____
_____
_____
_____
_____
_____

RECIPE: .... FROM: ....

SERVINGS: ...... PREP TIME: .... COOK TIME:.......... OVEN TEMP: ....

INGREDIENTS: _____

_____

_____

_____

_____

_____

_____

_____

_____

_____

_____

_____

_____

_____

_____

_____

INSTRUCTIONS: _____

_____

_____

_____

_____

_____

_____

_____

_____

_____

_____

_____

_____

RECIPE: .... FROM: ....

SERVINGS: ...... PREP TIME: .... COOK TIME:.......... OVEN TEMP: ....

INGREDIENTS: _____

_____

_____

_____

_____

_____

_____

_____

_____

_____

_____

_____

_____

_____

_____

INSTRUCTIONS: _____

_____

_____

_____

_____

_____

_____

_____

_____

_____

_____

_____

_____

_____

_____

RECIPE: .... FROM: ....

SERVINGS: ...... PREP TIME: .... COOK TIME:.......... OVEN TEMP: ....

INGREDIENTS: _____

_____
_____
_____
_____
_____
_____
_____
_____
_____
_____
_____
_____
_____
_____

INSTRUCTIONS: _____

_____
_____
_____
_____
_____
_____
_____
_____
_____
_____
_____
_____
_____
_____

RECIPE: .... FROM: ....

SERVINGS: ...... PREP TIME: .... COOK TIME:.......... OVEN TEMP: ....

INGREDIENTS: _____

_____

_____

_____

_____

_____

_____

_____

_____

_____

_____

_____

_____

_____

_____

INSTRUCTIONS: _____

_____

_____

_____

_____

_____

_____

_____

_____

_____

_____

_____

_____

_____

_____

RECIPE: .... FROM: ....

SERVINGS: ...... PREP TIME: .... COOK TIME:.......... OVEN TEMP: ....

INGREDIENTS: _____

_____

_____

_____

_____

_____

_____

_____

_____

_____

_____

_____

_____

_____

_____

_____

INSTRUCTIONS: _____

_____

_____

_____

_____

_____

_____

_____

_____

_____

_____

_____

_____

_____

_____

RECIPE: .... FROM: ....

SERVINGS: ...... PREP TIME: .... COOK TIME:.......... OVEN TEMP: ....

INGREDIENTS: _____

_____
_____
_____
_____
_____
_____
_____
_____
_____
_____
_____
_____
_____
_____
_____

INSTRUCTIONS: _____

_____
_____
_____
_____
_____
_____
_____
_____
_____
_____
_____
_____
_____
_____

RECIPE: .... FROM: ....

SERVINGS: ...... PREP TIME: .... COOK TIME:.......... OVEN TEMP: ....

INGREDIENTS: _____

_____

_____

_____

_____

_____

_____

_____

_____

_____

_____

_____

_____

_____

_____

_____

_____

INSTRUCTIONS: _____

_____

_____

_____

_____

_____

_____

_____

_____

_____

_____

_____

_____

_____

_____

RECIPE: .... FROM: ....

SERVINGS: ...... PREP TIME: .... COOK TIME:.......... OVEN TEMP: ....

INGREDIENTS: _____

_____
_____
_____
_____
_____
_____
_____
_____
_____
_____
_____
_____
_____
_____

INSTRUCTIONS: _____

_____
_____
_____
_____
_____
_____
_____
_____
_____
_____
_____
_____
_____
_____
_____

RECIPE: .... FROM: ....

SERVINGS: ...... PREP TIME: .... COOK TIME:.......... OVEN TEMP: ....

INGREDIENTS: _____

_____

_____

_____

_____

_____

_____

_____

_____

_____

_____

_____

_____

_____

_____

_____

_____

INSTRUCTIONS: _____

_____

_____

_____

_____

_____

_____

_____

_____

_____

_____

_____

_____

_____

_____

RECIPE: .... FROM: ....

SERVINGS: ...... PREP TIME: .... COOK TIME:.......... OVEN TEMP: ....

INGREDIENTS: _____

_____

_____

_____

_____

_____

_____

_____

_____

_____

_____

_____

_____

_____

_____

INSTRUCTIONS: _____

_____

_____

_____

_____

_____

_____

_____

_____

_____

_____

_____

_____

_____

RECIPE: .... FROM: ....

SERVINGS: ...... PREP TIME: .... COOK TIME:.......... OVEN TEMP: ....

INGREDIENTS: _____

_____
_____
_____
_____
_____
_____
_____
_____
_____
_____
_____
_____
_____
_____

INSTRUCTIONS: _____

_____
_____
_____
_____
_____
_____
_____
_____
_____
_____
_____
_____
_____
_____

RECIPE: .... FROM: ....

SERVINGS: ...... PREP TIME: .... COOK TIME:.......... OVEN TEMP: ....

INGREDIENTS: _____

_____
_____
_____
_____
_____
_____
_____
_____
_____
_____
_____
_____
_____
_____

INSTRUCTIONS: _____

_____
_____
_____
_____
_____
_____
_____
_____
_____
_____
_____
_____
_____
_____

RECIPE: .... FROM: ....

SERVINGS: ...... PREP TIME: .... COOK TIME:.......... OVEN TEMP: ....

INGREDIENTS: _____

_____

_____

_____

_____

_____

_____

_____

_____

_____

_____

_____

_____

_____

_____

INSTRUCTIONS: _____

_____

_____

_____

_____

_____

_____

_____

_____

_____

_____

_____

_____

_____

RECIPE: .... FROM: ....

SERVINGS: ...... PREP TIME: .... COOK TIME:.......... OVEN TEMP: ....

INGREDIENTS: _____

_____

_____

_____

_____

_____

_____

_____

_____

_____

_____

_____

_____

_____

_____

INSTRUCTIONS: _____

_____

_____

_____

_____

_____

_____

_____

_____

_____

_____

_____

_____

_____

_____

RECIPE: .... FROM: ....

SERVINGS: ...... PREP TIME: .... COOK TIME:.......... OVEN TEMP: ....

INGREDIENTS: _____

_____

_____

_____

_____

_____

_____

_____

_____

_____

_____

_____

_____

_____

_____

INSTRUCTIONS: _____

_____

_____

_____

_____

_____

_____

_____

_____

_____

_____

_____

_____

_____

RECIPE: .... FROM: ....

SERVINGS: ...... PREP TIME: .... COOK TIME:.......... OVEN TEMP: ....

INGREDIENTS: _____

_____

_____

_____

_____

_____

_____

_____

_____

_____

_____

_____

_____

_____

INSTRUCTIONS: _____

_____

_____

_____

_____

_____

_____

_____

_____

_____

_____

_____

_____

_____

RECIPE: .... FROM: ....

SERVINGS: ...... PREP TIME: .... COOK TIME:.......... OVEN TEMP: ....

INGREDIENTS: _____

_____

_____

_____

_____

_____

_____

_____

_____

_____

_____

_____

_____

_____

_____

_____

_____

INSTRUCTIONS: _____

_____

_____

_____

_____

_____

_____

_____

_____

_____

_____

_____

_____

_____

_____

RECIPE: .... FROM: ....

SERVINGS: ...... PREP TIME: .... COOK TIME:.......... OVEN TEMP: ....

INGREDIENTS: _____

_____

_____

_____

_____

_____

_____

_____

_____

_____

_____

_____

_____

_____

INSTRUCTIONS: _____

_____

_____

_____

_____

_____

_____

_____

_____

_____

_____

_____

_____

RECIPE: .... FROM: ....

SERVINGS: ...... PREP TIME: .... COOK TIME:.......... OVEN TEMP: ....

INGREDIENTS: _____

_____

_____

_____

_____

_____

_____

_____

_____

_____

_____

_____

_____

_____

_____

INSTRUCTIONS: _____

_____

_____

_____

_____

_____

_____

_____

_____

_____

_____

_____

_____

RECIPE: .... FROM: ....

SERVINGS: ...... PREP TIME: .... COOK TIME:.......... OVEN TEMP: ....

INGREDIENTS: _____

_____

_____

_____

_____

_____

_____

_____

_____

_____

_____

_____

_____

_____

_____

INSTRUCTIONS: _____

_____

_____

_____

_____

_____

_____

_____

_____

_____

_____

_____

_____

_____

_____

RECIPE: .... FROM: ....

SERVINGS: ...... PREP TIME: .... COOK TIME:.......... OVEN TEMP: ....

INGREDIENTS: _____

_____

_____

_____

_____

_____

_____

_____

_____

_____

_____

_____

_____

_____

_____

INSTRUCTIONS: _____

_____

_____

_____

_____

_____

_____

_____

_____

_____

_____

_____

_____

_____

RECIPE: .... FROM: ....

SERVINGS: ...... PREP TIME: .... COOK TIME:.......... OVEN TEMP: ....

INGREDIENTS: _____

_____

_____

_____

_____

_____

_____

_____

_____

_____

_____

_____

_____

_____

_____

INSTRUCTIONS: _____

_____

_____

_____

_____

_____

_____

_____

_____

_____

_____

_____

_____

_____

_____

RECIPE: .... FROM: ....

SERVINGS: ...... PREP TIME: .... COOK TIME:.......... OVEN TEMP: ....

INGREDIENTS: _____

_____

_____

_____

_____

_____

_____

_____

_____

_____

_____

_____

_____

_____

_____

_____

INSTRUCTIONS: _____

_____

_____

_____

_____

_____

_____

_____

_____

_____

_____

_____

_____

_____

RECIPE: .... FROM: ....

SERVINGS: ...... PREP TIME: .... COOK TIME:.......... OVEN TEMP: ....

INGREDIENTS: _____

_____
_____
_____
_____
_____
_____
_____
_____
_____
_____
_____
_____
_____
_____

INSTRUCTIONS: _____

_____
_____
_____
_____
_____
_____
_____
_____
_____
_____
_____
_____
_____

RECIPE: .... FROM: ....

SERVINGS: ...... PREP TIME: .... COOK TIME:.......... OVEN TEMP: ....

INGREDIENTS: _____

_____

_____

_____

_____

_____

_____

_____

_____

_____

_____

_____

_____

_____

_____

INSTRUCTIONS: _____

_____

_____

_____

_____

_____

_____

_____

_____

_____

_____

_____

_____

RECIPE: .... FROM: ....

SERVINGS: ...... PREP TIME: .... COOK TIME:.......... OVEN TEMP: ....

INGREDIENTS: _____
_____
_____
_____
_____
_____
_____
_____
_____
_____
_____
_____
_____
_____
_____

INSTRUCTIONS: _____
_____
_____
_____
_____
_____
_____
_____
_____
_____
_____
_____
_____
_____
_____

RECIPE: .... FROM: ....

SERVINGS: ...... PREP TIME: .... COOK TIME:.......... OVEN TEMP: ....

INGREDIENTS: _____

_____
_____
_____
_____
_____
_____
_____
_____
_____
_____
_____
_____
_____
_____

INSTRUCTIONS: _____

_____
_____
_____
_____
_____
_____
_____
_____
_____
_____
_____
_____
_____
_____
_____

RECIPE: .... FROM: ....

SERVINGS: ...... PREP TIME: .... COOK TIME:.......... OVEN TEMP: ....

INGREDIENTS: _____

_____

_____

_____

_____

_____

_____

_____

_____

_____

_____

_____

_____

_____

_____

INSTRUCTIONS: _____

_____

_____

_____

_____

_____

_____

_____

_____

_____

_____

_____

_____

_____

RECIPE: .... FROM: ....

SERVINGS: ...... PREP TIME: .... COOK TIME:.......... OVEN TEMP: ....

INGREDIENTS: _____

_____

_____

_____

_____

_____

_____

_____

_____

_____

_____

_____

_____

_____

_____

INSTRUCTIONS: _____

_____

_____

_____

_____

_____

_____

_____

_____

_____

_____

_____

_____

_____

RECIPE: .... FROM: ....

SERVINGS: ...... PREP TIME: .... COOK TIME:.......... OVEN TEMP: ....

INGREDIENTS: _____

_____
_____
_____
_____
_____
_____
_____
_____
_____
_____
_____
_____
_____

INSTRUCTIONS: _____

_____
_____
_____
_____
_____
_____
_____
_____
_____
_____
_____
_____
_____
_____

RECIPE: .... FROM: ....

SERVINGS: ...... PREP TIME: .... COOK TIME: .... OVEN TEMP: ....

INGREDIENTS: _____

_____

_____

_____

_____

_____

_____

_____

_____

_____

_____

_____

_____

_____

_____

_____

INSTRUCTIONS: _____

_____

_____

_____

_____

_____

_____

_____

_____

_____

_____

_____

_____

_____

_____

RECIPE: .... FROM: ....

SERVINGS: ...... PREP TIME: .... COOK TIME:.......... OVEN TEMP: ....

INGREDIENTS: _____

_____

_____

_____

_____

_____

_____

_____

_____

_____

_____

_____

_____

_____

_____

INSTRUCTIONS: _____

_____

_____

_____

_____

_____

_____

_____

_____

_____

_____

_____

_____

_____

RECIPE: .... FROM: ....

SERVINGS: ...... PREP TIME: .... COOK TIME:.......... OVEN TEMP: ....

INGREDIENTS: _____

_____

_____

_____

_____

_____

_____

_____

_____

_____

_____

_____

_____

_____

_____

INSTRUCTIONS: _____

_____

_____

_____

_____

_____

_____

_____

_____

_____

_____

_____

_____

_____

RECIPE: .... FROM: ....

SERVINGS: ...... PREP TIME: .... COOK TIME:.......... OVEN TEMP: ....

INGREDIENTS: _____

_____

_____

_____

_____

_____

_____

_____

_____

_____

_____

_____

_____

_____

_____

INSTRUCTIONS: _____

_____

_____

_____

_____

_____

_____

_____

_____

_____

_____

_____

_____

_____

RECIPE: .... FROM: ....

SERVINGS: ...... PREP TIME: .... COOK TIME:.......... OVEN TEMP: ....

INGREDIENTS: _____

_____

_____

_____

_____

_____

_____

_____

_____

_____

_____

_____

_____

_____

_____

INSTRUCTIONS: _____

_____

_____

_____

_____

_____

_____

_____

_____

_____

_____

_____

_____

RECIPE: .... FROM: ....

SERVINGS: ...... PREP TIME: .... COOK TIME:.......... OVEN TEMP: ....

INGREDIENTS: _____

_____

_____

_____

_____

_____

_____

_____

_____

_____

_____

_____

_____

_____

_____

INSTRUCTIONS: _____

_____

_____

_____

_____

_____

_____

_____

_____

_____

_____

_____

_____

_____

_____

RECIPE: .... FROM: ....

SERVINGS: ...... PREP TIME: .... COOK TIME:.......... OVEN TEMP: ....

INGREDIENTS: _____

_____

_____

_____

_____

_____

_____

_____

_____

_____

_____

_____

_____

_____

_____

INSTRUCTIONS: _____

_____

_____

_____

_____

_____

_____

_____

_____

_____

_____

_____

_____

RECIPE: .... FROM: ....

SERVINGS: ...... PREP TIME: .... COOK TIME:.......... OVEN TEMP: ....

INGREDIENTS: _____

_____

_____

_____

_____

_____

_____

_____

_____

_____

_____

_____

_____

_____

INSTRUCTIONS: _____

_____

_____

_____

_____

_____

_____

_____

_____

_____

_____

_____

_____

_____

RECIPE: .... FROM: ....

SERVINGS: ...... PREP TIME: .... COOK TIME:.......... OVEN TEMP: ....

INGREDIENTS: _____

_____

_____

_____

_____

_____

_____

_____

_____

_____

_____

_____

_____

_____

_____

INSTRUCTIONS: _____

_____

_____

_____

_____

_____

_____

_____

_____

_____

_____

_____

_____

RECIPE: .... FROM: ....

SERVINGS: ...... PREP TIME: .... COOK TIME:.......... OVEN TEMP: ....

INGREDIENTS: _____

_____

_____

_____

_____

_____

_____

_____

_____

_____

_____

_____

_____

INSTRUCTIONS: _____

_____

_____

_____

_____

_____

_____

_____

_____

_____

_____

_____

_____

_____

RECIPE: .... FROM: ....

SERVINGS: ...... PREP TIME: .... COOK TIME:.......... OVEN TEMP: ....

INGREDIENTS: _____

_____

_____

_____

_____

_____

_____

_____

_____

_____

_____

_____

_____

_____

_____

_____

INSTRUCTIONS: _____

_____

_____

_____

_____

_____

_____

_____

_____

_____

_____

_____

_____

_____

RECIPE: .... FROM: ....

SERVINGS: ...... PREP TIME: .... COOK TIME:.......... OVEN TEMP: ....

INGREDIENTS: _____

_____

_____

_____

_____

_____

_____

_____

_____

_____

_____

_____

_____

_____

INSTRUCTIONS: _____

_____

_____

_____

_____

_____

_____

_____

_____

_____

_____

_____

_____

RECIPE: .... FROM: ....

SERVINGS: ...... PREP TIME: .... COOK TIME: .... OVEN TEMP: ....

INGREDIENTS: _____

_____

_____

_____

_____

_____

_____

_____

_____

_____

_____

_____

_____

_____

_____

_____

INSTRUCTIONS: _____

_____

_____

_____

_____

_____

_____

_____

_____

_____

_____

_____

_____

_____

RECIPE: .... FROM: ....

SERVINGS: ...... PREP TIME: .... COOK TIME:.......... OVEN TEMP: ....

INGREDIENTS: _____

_____

_____

_____

_____

_____

_____

_____

_____

_____

_____

_____

_____

_____

INSTRUCTIONS: _____

_____

_____

_____

_____

_____

_____

_____

_____

_____

_____

_____

_____

_____

RECIPE: .... FROM: ....

SERVINGS: ...... PREP TIME: .... COOK TIME:.......... OVEN TEMP: ....

INGREDIENTS: _____

_____

_____

_____

_____

_____

_____

_____

_____

_____

_____

_____

_____

_____

_____

INSTRUCTIONS: _____

_____

_____

_____

_____

_____

_____

_____

_____

_____

_____

_____

_____

_____

_____

RECIPE: .... FROM: ....

SERVINGS: ...... PREP TIME: .... COOK TIME:.......... OVEN TEMP: ....

INGREDIENTS: _____

_____

_____

_____

_____

_____

_____

_____

_____

_____

_____

_____

_____

_____

INSTRUCTIONS: _____

_____

_____

_____

_____

_____

_____

_____

_____

_____

_____

_____

_____

RECIPE: .... FROM: ....

SERVINGS: ...... PREP TIME: .... COOK TIME:.......... OVEN TEMP: ....

INGREDIENTS: _____

_____

_____

_____

_____

_____

_____

_____

_____

_____

_____

_____

_____

_____

INSTRUCTIONS: _____

_____

_____

_____

_____

_____

_____

_____

_____

_____

_____

_____

_____

_____

RECIPE: .... FROM: ....

SERVINGS: ...... PREP TIME: .... COOK TIME:.......... OVEN TEMP: ....

INGREDIENTS: _____

_____

_____

_____

_____

_____

_____

_____

_____

_____

_____

_____

_____

INSTRUCTIONS: _____

_____

_____

_____

_____

_____

_____

_____

_____

_____

_____

_____

_____

_____

_____

RECIPE: .... FROM: ....

SERVINGS: ...... PREP TIME: .... COOK TIME:.......... OVEN TEMP: ....

INGREDIENTS: _____

_____

_____

_____

_____

_____

_____

_____

_____

_____

_____

_____

_____

_____

INSTRUCTIONS: _____

_____

_____

_____

_____

_____

_____

_____

_____

_____

_____

_____

_____

RECIPE: .... FROM: ....

SERVINGS: ...... PREP TIME: .... COOK TIME:.......... OVEN TEMP: ....

INGREDIENTS: _____

_____

_____

_____

_____

_____

_____

_____

_____

_____

_____

_____

_____

_____

INSTRUCTIONS: _____

_____

_____

_____

_____

_____

_____

_____

_____

_____

_____

_____

_____

_____

_____

RECIPE: .... FROM: ....

SERVINGS: ...... PREP TIME: .... COOK TIME:.......... OVEN TEMP: ....

INGREDIENTS: _____

_____

_____

_____

_____

_____

_____

_____

_____

_____

_____

_____

_____

_____

_____

INSTRUCTIONS: _____

_____

_____

_____

_____

_____

_____

_____

_____

_____

_____

_____

_____

_____

RECIPE: .... FROM: ....

SERVINGS: ...... PREP TIME: .... COOK TIME:.......... OVEN TEMP: ....

INGREDIENTS: _____

_____

_____

_____

_____

_____

_____

_____

_____

_____

_____

_____

_____

_____

INSTRUCTIONS: _____

_____

_____

_____

_____

_____

_____

_____

_____

_____

_____

_____

_____

_____

RECIPE: .... FROM: ....

SERVINGS: ...... PREP TIME: .... COOK TIME:.......... OVEN TEMP: ....

INGREDIENTS: _____

_____
_____
_____
_____
_____
_____
_____
_____
_____
_____
_____
_____
_____
_____
_____

INSTRUCTIONS: _____

_____
_____
_____
_____
_____
_____
_____
_____
_____
_____
_____
_____
_____

RECIPE: .... FROM: ....

SERVINGS: ...... PREP TIME: .... COOK TIME:.......... OVEN TEMP: ....

INGREDIENTS: _____

_____

_____

_____

_____

_____

_____

_____

_____

_____

_____

_____

_____

INSTRUCTIONS: _____

_____

_____

_____

_____

_____

_____

_____

_____

_____

_____

_____

_____

_____

RECIPE: .... FROM: ....

SERVINGS: ...... PREP TIME: .... COOK TIME:.......... OVEN TEMP: ....

INGREDIENTS: _____

_____

_____

_____

_____

_____

_____

_____

_____

_____

_____

_____

_____

_____

_____

INSTRUCTIONS: _____

_____

_____

_____

_____

_____

_____

_____

_____

_____

_____

_____

_____

RECIPE: .... FROM: ....

SERVINGS: ...... PREP TIME: .... COOK TIME:.......... OVEN TEMP: ....

INGREDIENTS: _____

_____

_____

_____

_____

_____

_____

_____

_____

_____

_____

_____

_____

INSTRUCTIONS: _____

_____

_____

_____

_____

_____

_____

_____

_____

_____

_____

_____

Made in the USA
San Bernardino, CA
23 November 2019